Part 1: Toxic Love

1. Toxic Love
2. Stay Away From Me
3. Take You Back
4. Letting You Go
5. Toxic Love
6. Drink You Away
7. Nothing Kills You Like A Broken Heart
8. Friend
9. Are You Out There?
10. Fight For Me
11. Fool
12. Goodbye

Toxic Love

They say that you will be the death of me.
They say that you will be the end of me.
But I say that I just can't get enough of you!

I should say no.
I should just walk away.
But you have a hold on me and you won't let go!
I guess that I'm here to stay.

This kind of love isn't good for anyone.
Somehow we just can't seem to let go.
I have a feeling that you will always be the one.
No matter how much my head is telling me no.

You're a toxic kind of love and I will never let you go!
Though it would be the making of me, I will never let you go!

For some reason I really can't get enough of you.
You are the worst and best I've ever had.
Why do I stay? I really have no clue.
You can make me the happiest and yet nobody's ever made me more sad.

We fight then we break up and you drive me insane.
Then I'll give in and we do it all over again.

You are my toxic lover but one day you will no longer be!
Never again in my tears, heart or mind.
We will become strangers and we will no longer be!

Toxic Lover Goodbye!
For you I will no longer cry!

Stay Away From Me

I'm begging you just please.
Just please stay away from me.
Even though I try my best to.
I just can't resist you.
So stay away from me.

We have been down this path before.
Never changing lanes.
Expecting something different.
But everything stays the same.

Because even though I will it not to.
My heart belongs to you.
There's nothing I can do.

So I'm begging you just please.
Stay away from me!
Even though I try my best to.
I just can't resist you.
Stay away from me!

There's only so many mistakes before lessons need to be learned.
Even though it's broken we keep trying to fix it.
Leaving nothing but our own misery.
Holding onto hopes of something we can never be.

I keep saying this will be the last time.
But then we hit repeat.
It's like we do the same damn thing.
And yet we wonder why this keeps happening.

We were never meant to be!
But in my heart it's you I always see!

You're not what I should want.
We are not what we need.
If love's a drug, then I'm addicted.
It's about time for my recovery.

Forget our feelings and face the truth!
What we have will never do!

So I'm begging you just please.
Stay away from me!
Even though I try my best to.

The Inside Look

I just can't resist you.
Stay away from me!

Part One: Toxic Love

Take You Back

You must be mad if you think I'd just take you back.
After all the shit you pulled I deserve more than that.
I would be mad if I was ever going to take you back.
There's no going back, I'm so over that!

You played me like a fool the whole time we were together.
I deserve better than that!
You only seen me as time to pass when I thought that we were forever.
I deserve better than that!

I was a fool to believe all the lies you said.
I was a fool to go along with all the games you played.
But I'm not your fool anymore and you can no longer play with my head!
Because now I'd never take you back, not even if I was paid.

I'll never take you back!
I deserve so much more than you.
I'd be mad if I ever took you back.
I will find a better love than you.
I'll never take you back!

Letting You Go

All those games you keep on playing are leaving me so confused.
I'm growing so sick of trying to figure out what's real with you and what's only for your show.
You used to make me feel special but now I only feel used.
I hope your happy playing your games because now I'm letting you go.

I can't take this anymore so I've got to let you go.
All this confusion is killing me.
I've got to say no!
It's time for me to be free.

I never wanted to love you and now I don't think I will stop.
But I'm learning to move on from you.
I may love your highs but I can't take another drop.
I gave you so many chances but you will never change the things you do.

I'm letting you go can't take this no more!
I'm letting you go I don't feel like I did before!
I'm letting you go because I deserve so much more!

You Don't Love Me

I used to think that you were the one.
Thought we would be together until the very end.
But now I've realised you were only sticking around for the fun.
Should have known better than to think you'd ever be a perfect boyfriend.

You don't love me and it tears me apart.
You don't love me and it breaks my heart.

There was a time where you were all I could see.
I never thought I'd love anyone the way I loved you.
But now I finally see that we were never meant to be.
Maybe one day I'll finally find someone true.

How could I have not seen all the warning signs that were staring at me?
How could I be stupid enough to let you in?
You were meant to be my happy ending but you only brought me misery.
I'm starting to see now that loving you is my greatest sin.

I gave you everything I had in me but you never felt the same.
I let you in not knowing that you never planned to stay.
Our love was just a lie and I was a fool while you played me like a game.
But the game is over now and losing you is the price I am ready to pay.

Why couldn't I see the truth from the start?
Why did I let you waste my time?
How could I give away my heart?
Loving you should be a crime!

You never cared and you never loved me.
You just wanted someone to want you.
I was somebody to waste time with and that's all you could see.
I was so stupid to think otherwise I never had a clue.

You don't love me and I'm not your fool anymore!
You don't love me and your games no longer work on me anymore!
In time I will no longer love you!
Now I know our love was never true!

Drink You Away

Put another vodka in my glass.
No longer going to care about his ass.
Second thoughts better make it a double.
I can tell we are going to be heading for trouble.

I'm going to get my best clothes on and forget all about you.
I'm so over this, you and me are through.
Time for drinking away the sorrows and to dance like nobody's watching me.
For everyone whose watching I'm going to give them the best entertainment they will ever see!

Shots did someone say there's a shot?
Go on mister barman and give me all that you've got.
I'm ready to party until he is out of my head.
Get so drunk and maybe even jump into a stranger's bed.

Whisky?
No need to frisk me!
Just put it in my glass and go on your way.
I'm going to party until night turns into day.

He said without him there's no me.
Well we will just wait and see.
Now that the drinks are flowing.
Memories of him are going!

Going to drink a fancy cocktail even though I don't know it's name.
Going to have some fun and give someone else the blame.
Your time is done boy I'm drinking you away.
Just like this impending hangover you are not here to stay!

Nothing Kills You Like A Broken Heart

I swore that I'd never give into love.
But you were my only exception.
I thought I was too smart to give into love.
But I was fooled by your deception.

You left me lying alone feeling broken and forgotten.
Still wanting you but at the same time hating you.
You left me feeling like my heart was rotten.
The tears kept falling despite how hard I fought for them not to.

I guess it's true what they all say.
Trust me to have to learn it the hard way.
Nothing kills you like a broken heart!
You tore me apart.

I was never one to believe in the happy ever after.
But for a moment you made me believe it.
If only I knew the truth behind what you were after.

Nothing kills you like a broken heart!
How do you heal when you've been torn apart?

Never looked for love but it somehow came and found me.
I really believed that you were the one.
To all your lies I was just too blind to see.
Now you've left me broken and undone.

Someone please tell me what am I supposed to do?
When the one you love tears you in two.
What am I supposed to do?
When nothing feels like it used to.

Yes, it's true what they all say.
I had to learn it the hard way.
Nothing kills you like a broken heart!
All that we had he just took and tore apart.

Friend

I need to find a way to hate you so I can find a way to quit you.
These illusions I've dreamt up between us will never become a reality.
Living on the what if and what could've been will never do.
I can no longer hold out for a hope of you and me.

Friendship turns to love everyday but you will never look at me that way.
I keep reading into signs that aren't even there just because I can't let you go.
I will never look at you as just a friend but you will only ever look at me that way.
Too free myself I need to let you go.

I'm sure that you love me but not in the way I want you to.
I can't hate you for not being able to love me.
But we can't stay friends when I want so much more from you.
I would do anything for you to open your eyes and see me.
In the way that I see you.

I've fooled myself for too long thinking you'd ever love me.
I've fooled myself into thinking that friends would ever be enough for me or you.
When you talk about the others it slowly kills me.
I've got to force myself to open my eyes and finally see what's true.

A friend is all I will ever be to you!
No matter how hard my heart pleads for this not to be true.
A friend is something I can no longer be to you!
I need to move on from my fantasies and find a love that's true.

Are You Out There?

I'm still waiting on my happy ending.
I'm still waiting for my mister right.
But all this waiting always comes to nothing.
You are just too far out of sight.

Are you even out there?
Or am I just waiting on a fantasy that will never come my way?
Happiness never seems to come here.
But I keep waiting for my perfect day.

I have been with quite a few.
But nothing ever works out for me.
No matter what I try and do.
They are just never right for me.

I can blame myself for asking for too much.
Or is love just enough?
A perfect life maybe asking for too much.
I just want a life that's not rough.

Everyone seems so happy why can't that be me?
I just want someone to love and treat me right.
A love like all the others that I see.
A love that's real and a guy that's right.

I'm tired of being lonely I just want someone to comfort me.
I just want my happy ending.
Why can't the one just find me?
I'm growing tired of waiting.

He's got to be able to put up with all the crazy little things that I do.
He's got to understand me and listen to the things that I say.
He can't be built on lies because I really need him to be true.
I want him to be grateful to have me every single day.

Are you out there mister right?
Hiding so good.
Hiding just out of sight.
Will you love me like I wish you would?

Fight For Me

You and I forever I've heard it all before.
All those painful little lies like I could only ever love you more and more.
But that never stops them walking out the door.

If you're in this then you better be in this for real!
I'm not giving my heart away to another lie.
If you're in this then you're going to have to feel what I feel.
If not, then we might as well say goodbye.

It's not going to be easy to convince me.
I've been hurt so many times before.
But if you're not willing to fight then you're not right for me.
I'm not longer giving my heart away so easily anymore.

If you're in this like you say you are then you've got to be ready to fight for me!
I won't give in so easily!
So if you want me then fight for me!
You've got to prove I can trust you and you'd be true to me.

I'm going to be a whole lot of work but for the right person I could be worth it.
I won't fight to keep you, if you want to go then go!
I've fought before for people who never gave a shit.
If you're not ready to fight for me then get ready to go!

I won't fight for you!
You've got to fight for me!
It will be easy if your love is really true.
If you're not willing to fight for me then allow me to be free.

There's only so many times you can break before you begin struggling to heal.
There's only so many fights before you lose yourself in the heartache.
I am a lot to take on so you got to be able to deal.
Because I refuse to allow myself to head for another heartbreak.

Get ready to fight for me or get ready to let me go!
I won't settle for anything less when I deserve so much more.
Get ready to fight for me or get ready to let me go!
I won't fight for you; I'll just show you the door.

Fool

You looked at me with those innocent eyes as if you could do no wrong.
You spoke to me in ways that made me feel like you were someone I could rely on.
You fooled me with your lies making me think that we were strong.
But you were full of lies and I should've realized that you would soon be gone.

Go ahead and spread those lies making me out to be the bad one.
If it makes it easier for you to play the victim, then don't let me stop you.
We both know the truth and no matter what you say that can't be undone.
You'll be living in regret and they'll all see through you.

I thought you were the greatest but you turned out to be the worst!
I thought you were a friend I could trust but you were just waiting for your time to turn.
You act like you're selfless but you are always going to put yourself first.
I was foolish enough to think our friendship meant something but you just stood there and let it burn.

Consider me dead to you because you killed any connection we ever had.
It's too late now for apologies because you mean nothing to me now!
You've lost because you never knew the true friend that you had.

Go ahead and play your games to some other fool.
In the end you will always lose because there's nothing inside you that's ever true!
Go ahead and spread your hate because you'll soon realize you are the only fool.

Goodbye

Haven't we both been here before?
Why do we keep trying to recapture this dwindling flame?
We keep trying to find the magic when there's nothing left here anymore.
Our love has died and we've only got ourselves to blame.

I remember when even the thought of you used to fill my day with joy.
I remember when a day without you seemed like forever.
But something's gone wrong and we've lost our joy.
It's time we realized that we can't hold on to the past forever.

When the love has gone it's not going to come back.
There's no use fighting the truth when it's plain for us to see.
We are so far off this path that there's no going back on track.
It's time for us to both be free.

We've both been trying so hard but I can't give anymore.
There is nothing left for us to keep fighting for.
We need to call it quits and walk out the door.
We both deserve so much more!

I don't want to be without you!
But being with you when the love has gone wouldn't be true.
I don't know how to be without you!
But this is something we both have to do.

For a time, you were the one and I thought you always would be.
But somehow we lost the love along the way.
It's time to face the facts that you no longer love me.
We'd only be hurting ourselves if we were foolish enough to stay.

Our love has died and it can't be revived.

We have got to be strong enough to say goodbye.
There is nothing left for us to save.
There's no more tears for us to dry.
It's time for us to say goodbye! It's time for us to be brave!

Part 2: Unforgiven

1. Unforgiven
2. Time Stands Still
3. Scars Of My Past
4. Don’t Leave Me
5. Wish You Were Dead
6. Keep Coming Back
7. Lies
8. Never A Victim
9. Care
10. Fight Back
11. After The Storm

Unforgiven

They say that forgiveness can be the path to a man's full recovery.
But what can you do if you can't forgive?
If your mind has been poisoned for so long that hatred is all you can see?
If no matter what you can't let go of your past and your struggling just to live?

Your poison came into my life and within that moment you ended it.
My innocence forever gone.
Your poison ripped through my life and with your actions you ended it.
How could somebody be so wrong?

How could someone who you're supposed to trust be so cruel and bad?
How could you do the things you did to me?
How can even the thought of you after all this time still make me so sad?
Pain is all I feel and the memories are all I see.

I can't and I won't forgive you for what you have done!
I don't think I will ever let go of the pain you brought on me.
Those things you did just can't come undone.
You turned my life into nothing but misery.

You took all that you could get and you left me for dead.
Broke me into pieces of a person I used to know.
Because of you I can't even look at myself without a feeling of dread.
I'm come to learn to live with being haunted for the rest of my life and that my pain will never go.

I will always hate you for what you did to me.
You've damaged me in ways that can't be repaired.
How can you live and lie about what you did to me?
You are the greatest darkness in my life the one I've always feared.

How can you play the victim after all you put me through?
You have the nerve to act like your innocent in every single way.
How can you live with the person that you are and the things only we know you do?
There has to be a time where you meet your judgement day.

You are and always will be unforgiven and that's the way it should be!
You will never understand the evil you are to me.
You don't deserve anything from me.
I don't want or need your apology!

One day your evil will be broadcast for everyone to see.
One day you will completely lose your twisted grip on me.

Time Stands Still

Every day it's repeated and every day I am defeated.
How can you lose it all when you started with nothing at all?
Every single day I force myself to fight even when I struggle to see the light.
But how can you win a war that starts at your own door?

Since that day my innocence was taken away, everything stays the same.
Time Stands Still.
Since that day I've been the one to blame.
Time Stands Still.
I'm stuck on repeat and it's killing me.
Time Stands Still.
I don't see how you get to be happy.

The hardest thing in my life wasn't to come clean and admit it all.
It was when you lied and covered up your sin.
You got it all and relished to see me fall.
You made me feel like the garbage that belonged in the bin.

You can fool them all with that devil smile but I am no longer a fool.
Your day is coming, evil can't stay hidden.
They may think that you're kind but nobody knows better than me that you're cruel.
You'll take what you can get, destroy what you may, to you nothing is forbidden!

Time Stands Still.
Day by day I remember it all.
Time Stands Still.
Day by day I remember all the things you made me do while under your thrall.

Memories can't be washed away no matter how hard you try.
There's some dirt that will stay with you until your grave!
One day you are going to trip up on your own lie.
You may think that I'm still weak, but I have had no choice but to become brave.

How could you do what you did to someone you were supposed to love?
What kind of monster gets off on all the pain they've caused and doesn't let it bother them?
You used me, abused me and made everyone feel like I was just something to get rid of.
You forced me to be on the outside all alone but you're the one whose scum.

Time Stands Still.
Since the day you took my innocence away.
Time Stands Still.
My life is stuck on repeat day after day.

You know what you did even though you struggle to admit anything at all.

But for me to survive this, I just got to believe that karma is coming for you.
If I'm strong enough to be patient the day will come that I get to see you fall.
The truth is catching up and there's nothing you can do!

The hardest thing isn't surviving the pain you have inflicted on me.
The hardest thing is learning how to deal with each day that comes after that.
Learning how to overcome what you did and not let it break me.
Struggling to understand how anyone could do something like that.

You are the monster under my bed.
You are the nightmare I will never forget!
You are the darkest voices in my head.
But remember just one thing, as long as I'm still breathing you haven't defeated me yet!

I believe that one day maybe soon or years away, your day will come!
You will realise the true monster you have become!

I hope that when that day comes you're stuck with only your lies.
I hope that your Time Stands Still.
That you are forced to relive the torture you have inflicted on other's lives.
I hope you go to your own hell and Time Stands Still!

Scars Of My Past

I'm so sick of this same dismal feeling.
I want to just run away.
But no amount of miles with help me with my healing.
Why can't this pain just go away?

I want some happiness instead of never ending pain.
I keep on trying to escape my past.
I'm feeling like I'm going insane.
Hoping one day for a love that will last.

Wish I could just wipe away the memories that are haunting me.
These scars of my past stop me from moving on.
Should be looking to a future but ghosts are all I see.
I need to hold on to some hope but I fear that it's all gone.

I'm so desperate to break free from my misery.
But it's all I seem to know.
Who I am today is not who I want to be.

All I want is to find a way to let go of the scars of my past.
All I want is to find a happiness that will last.

Don't Leave Me

How could the future that we were building turn out to be nothing but a lie?
How can you say you no longer love me when I know I will never stop loving you?
How could the love we shared just wither away and die?
I would do anything to stop you leaving, please just tell me what to do.

Don't let this be over aren't we worth the fight?
I have never stopped loving you, please don't stop loving me.
A life without you will never seem right.
Were you always planning to leave and I was just too blind to see?

Did I do something wrong because I know I can fix it.
Don't Leave Me!
If your love for me is broken maybe time can fix it.
Don't Leave Me!

We were so happy at the beginning please don't let this be the end.
Just tell me what I need to do because I can't lose you.
I don't want to lose a lover and a best friend.
Please don't let this be over, please don't let this be true.

Wish You Were Dead

You are the evil that has cursed my life!
I long for the day that you feel the strife.
I'm longing for the day that pain will be all you feel.
I keep wishing you dead and that your death will be painful and real!

One day you will pay for what you did to me.
One day the real you everyone will see.
Judgement day is coming for you!
Cursing you will be the last thing I do.

I have nothing left but hatred for you.
You and every poisonous little thing you do.
You take lives and you tear them apart.
Instead of regretting you just hit restart.

I wish you were dead!
I wish you got what was coming to you.
I wish you were dead!
Then there'd be no one you could tear into.

You are full of hate and despair.
I'm sick of being a victim to your lies.
You have taught me how life can be so cruel and unfair.
I can't wait for your demise!

As long as you are living you will carry on spreading your hate.
Taking all your poison and ruining people's lives.
Anyone who cares for you has a doomed fate.
You don't think twice about ruining lives.

You are the evil that has cursed my life and one day everyone will know!
I want to be the reason for your end.
If anyone is to be happy then you will need to go!
I keep cursing you, I keep longing for your evil to end.

I wish you were dead!
I wish you got what was coming to you.

All those lives ruined all because of you.
You don't even stop to care.
You just keep doing what comes natural to you.
The only way we will be happy is when you are no longer here.

You curse every life that you walk into.
You are barely a person, you're more like a bottle full of poison.

The Inside Look

The pain you inflict nobody can undo.
You will always live your life happily in sin.
Twisted games are all you know how to do.

There is no nice way of saying you wish someone would die.
But why play nice when it's something you will never do.
You broke me and made my life a lie.
People are nothing but victims to you.
I was nothing but a victim in your eye.

Keep Coming Back

I've hit the ground so many times before thinking that was the end of me.
But somehow I always survive.
The world keeps pulling me down but I never stop trying to break free.
In the end I know I will thrive!

Break these legs and I will learn how to walk again.
Break my heart and I will learn how to love again.

Even at my worst I'll keep coming back.
There will be no stopping me.
I will keep coming back.
You will never see the end of me!

I may get down in the gutter but it won't be long until I'm seeing the stars.
I will get lost but I will always find my way.
Lock me up and I will break through those bars.
There's no stopping me because I am here to stay!

I know that if you want that picture perfect.
Then you must work for it.

Nothing will stop me from fighting through my darkest day.
I know I have so much more to give.
I will make it through in my own way.
I know I have so much more to live!

Hit me with your worst and I'll keep coming back.
I've been to hell and back and somehow I'm still here.
Nothing can stop me, nothing can top me, I'll keep coming back!

Lies

I can finally see through your deceiving eyes.
I'm losing count of all your lies.
All you do is line up those knives and wait for my back to turn.
It has taken me forever to finally learn.

When it comes to you I've finally realised why nobody stays and they always run.
I can't believe it's taken me this long to be finally done.
I can't help but laugh at the thought that you think you might have won.
When it comes to the end I will always have love and you will have none.

All you ever do is lie do you even know what's true?
You are being lost within your own lie, no-one will know the real you.
I pity the life you choose to lead.
It's far too late now for you to ever be freed.

Your life has become a lie you have made.
I wouldn't change places with you no matter how much I was paid.
You have really come to believe that you have it all.
You can't even see that you're heading for a mighty fall.

Lies are all you live and breathe.
Too many lies which you can't reprieve.
You can't get to me anymore; I have come to know all of your lies.
Be Gone! Forever! It's time for us to say our goodbyes!

Never A Victim

Life isn't easy so let's not say that it is!
People are going to try and break you down but you're not going to let them!
Life isn't easy and nobody says that it is!
People are going to try their best to knock you down but you're never going to let them!

They can try their hardest but we are never going to stop.
They will knock us down and we will rise again.
Because nobody knows their own strength until they face their first drop.
There is always strength to be found in surviving through pain.

Never A Victim always a Fighter!
We were born to survive.
Never A Victim always a Fighter!
Even through the hardest of times we were born to thrive.

We have all fallen down and we call all get back up again.
Nothing is too hard to overcome as long as you are willing to try.
Life can be full of happiness but you are always going to have to deal with some pain.
We are all far too strong to just give in, curl up and die!

So hold that head up high and never give up!
We can do anything as long as we don't back down.
We can survive anything if we never give up.
We can't back down!
We will never back down!

Never A Victim forever a fighter!
No matter what we may go through we were born to survive.
Never A Victim forever a fighter!
Even through the toughest of challenges we can still thrive!

Never Be A Victim!
Forever A Fighter!

Care

I have found myself alone again.
Struggling just to feel a thing.
I've been in so much pain.
I can no longer feel anything.

If this was you could you handle what I've been and still go through?
Because I don't think I can anymore.
Struggling day to day just to make it through.
Never knowing what to do.

I just want to care about something.
I just want to feel even if it's pain.
I just don't want to let this misery win.
It's time to stop feeling numb and embrace the pain.

I've been hiding my feelings for so long deep down inside.
That it feels like it's killed me and left me with nothing.
I'm getting so tired of always having to hide.
I've got to not let this darkness win.

Why do I find it so hard just to care?
Why cant I let someone help me through?
Why are feelings what I fear?
What am I supposed to do?

I have been knocked down so many times before.
I'm struggling just to stay on my feet.
I feel like I can't take no more.
It's like life has truly had me beat.

I want to simply just care and not be in misery.
But somewhere long ago I lost it all.
Now darkness is all I can see.
And those once closest to me just stand to watch me fall.

I keep waiting to feel something more but that day never comes.
I keep waiting to hear something that will make a change but I never hear a sound.
Got to fight back at what I feel is breaking me.
Will I ever be free?

So please just give me a reason to care.
A reason just to be here.
A reason to not let go.
A reason to let my feelings flow.
Please just give me a reason to care.

Fight Back

Sometimes you are going to have to fall.
Sometimes you are going to lose it all.
But when you do get back up, you have got to stand tall.
Sometimes people can make you feel like you are nothing but the secret is that you can have it all.

Get Up!
Fight Back!
Never Let Them Win!

There will be days where you will feel small.
There will be days when you feel like you're nothing at all.
But everyone can be special in their own way.
You just have to stay strong even on your darkest day.

We are made of steel.
We are forced to deal.
Don't be afraid to feel.
Because we all learn to heal.

You are so much stronger than you know.
Though at times you may not feel like this.
You've got so much strength from your head to toe.
You just got to see in yourself what others might miss.

Get Up!
Fight Back!
Never Let Them Win!

The world is filled with haters waiting to turn on you.
They will try their hardest to break you.
When this day comes there's only one thing you can do.

Fight Back and Never Let Them Win!
Fight Back!
Never Let Them Win!

When we fall we get back up.
We will take and blow and then we will let them have another go.
Deep down we all know we can get back up.
We all have so much more power than we will ever know.

We are made of steel.
We are forced to deal.
Don't be afraid to feel.

Because we all learn to heal.

Get Up!
Fight Back!
Never Let Them Win!

Always Keep Fighting Back!
They Will Never Win!

After The Storm

I have fought for as long as I have lived.
I've stayed strong because I had no choice but to fight.
I've lived through the darkest days of my life and I survived.
I've forced myself to keep going on even when I couldn't see the light.

They say the worst thing about the storm is learning how to face it.
But how can you overcome the storm when it's all you've ever known?
They say the worst thing about the storm is learning how to embrace it.
But the worst thing about the storm is the aftermath of walking into the unknown.

I'm a natural born fighter who struggles to work out how to win their biggest fight.
I'm a survivor who only seems to know how to survive.
I may have faced some of my darkest fears but what comes after the storm remains the biggest fright.
I've been scraping by for so long I have forgotten how to live.

Does anybody really know what to do?
What to do when the storm is through with you?
I've dreamed many dreams about life after the storm but now I'm struggling to see what's left of me.
Have I got used to my own misery?

What does a fighter do when they no longer need to fight?
What does a survivor do when they have survived the worst that has come?
Is there any peace after the storm? Will I find the light?
Or is there just another storm making it's way home?

Finale Part 3: The Inner True Self

1. The Inner True Self
2. Let You In
3. Me
4. Get Over You
5. Erase You
6. Cry (The Unpoetic Poem)
7. Open The Doors
8. You Rock My World
9. Together We Fall
10. Take What You Got
11. Ultimate Me

The Inner True Self

The inner true self is what we all look to find.
A hidden potential or something that makes them shine bright.
To put their troubles behind.
Letting go of the dark and stepping into the light.

The conquest however is not as easy as it may seem.
No matter the struggle the end result is a need.
Achieving one's goals and brining life to the dream.
Anything it takes in-order to succeed.

We all ask the question who I am.
I am neither my past or my present.
That my friend is one mighty scam.
We all ask the question who I am.
But nobody ever knows the answer's complete content.

We can go on to hate who we are now.
To hate the pain and misery that we have been through.
But the pain will go, to this I vow.
And to our pasts we will all stand tall and embrace the things that have made you you.

The inner true self is what we all look to find.
To find who we are and to this we nurture.
But now I plead that you may be refined.
For history is what makes our future.

You mustn't hate where you are now.
For even the worst will help make you really you.
The pains of yesterday will slip away in a silent bow.

Till the day you can really say who am I?
I am me, perfect me! To which I know is no lie.
Despite the days when I struggled to get by.

So don't hate the life you are living now because one day it will bring you happiness.
Trust me and soon you shall see.
There truly is a way out of your misery.

Let You In

Please can I just deactivate this?
I don't want to be anywhere near it.
Love never works out for me so please can't I just give it a miss?
Take away my feelings because when it comes to my heart I will happily forfeit.

You are so dangerous making me feeling things that I have been hiding from for so many years.
I can't be anywhere near you because I refuse to let myself feel.
Feelings only lead to heartbreak and tears.
Letting people in has only ever lead to wounds that will never heal.

You seem pretty perfect but use all do at first.
I won't let you in because I can't take the pain.
You could be the one or you could be my latest bust.
My heart has been broken and I'll never let it happen.

My feelings for you I'll find a way to quit.
These walls I've build will never let you in.
These walls I've build will never submit.
I will learn to forget you; I will never let you in.

Don't bother wasting your time on me.
I will never change for you!
You can stop trying and you can be free.
You will find yourself somebody new, they always do.

Love is a fool's game that I only ever lose.
Love is a weakness just waiting to break you.
Love leads to heartbreak and leaves you with the blues.
Once you give into love there's nothing you can do!

A part of me would love to let you in but I know I never will.
I wish I could be strong enough to risk it all.
I can't let you in and I never will!
I'm not strong enough to survive another fall.

Me

I'm so done with everyone having an opinion about me.
When they don't even know half the shit that I've been through.
People are often too quick to judge by what they think they know or see.
I'm done trying to change opinions, at least I know what is true.

I'm so done with everyone judging me.
Fuck you to all my haters!
No one's going to stop me being me.

All you bitches must be tripping if you think you will bring me down.
No matter how hard I always rise when I fall.
I will never stay down!
I may never have it all but I will always be standing tall.

I am going to be living my life the only way I know how.
So you can all keep on judging it no longer bothers me.
The past will stay where it's meant to be left, I'm living for the now!

Get Over You

You can't fix what's been broken by adding a little glue.
You can't unsay what's been said with a worthless apology.
You've messed up for the last time and there's nothing you can do.
It's your loss because you will never find another me!

I've wasted far too much time on you.
It's time that I move on to something new.
It's time that I get over you!

I'm so sick of you filling my every thought when my life should be so much more.
I'm tired of waiting for you to open your eyes and realize I'm the one.
Time for you to walk out that door.
Time for me to finally find the one.

I've got to stay strong!
I deserve so much more than what you are able to give.
I've got to carry on!
You've got to let me live.

It's time for me to get over you!
There's nothing left to save.
It's time for me to get over you!
Please let me be brave.

Erase You

I keep trying to erase you.
But I can't seem to forget you.
Even though my heart tells me that I need to.
I just can't seem to find a way to erase you.

Take away these memories before they cripple me.
Take away these feelings before I get lost in them.
All that's left is the misery and I just need to be free.
Take away my rusting heart that you were so happy to condemn.

I just want to erase any memory of you.
Because it's killing me to keep holding onto yesterday.
If I can't have you anymore then I don't want any memory of you.
I can't keep holding onto hopes of you coming back one day.

The day you left you took my heart away.
Leaving me in pieces thinking of what could've been.
I would've done anything for you to stay.
But a happy ending for us is something you never seen.

I keep reliving the days when we were happy.
When all you wanted was to be with me.
When we were foolishly in love, so happy and free.
Why did you have to go and leave me?

These memories are useless if I can't share them with you!
All they do is remind me of how stupid I was to let you go.
I can't keep living with our history I just want to erase you!
Living with these memories are more painful than you could ever know!

Cry (The Unpoetic Poem)

I used to cry myself to sleep at night.
Calling for you.
Missing you.

Years may have gone by now.
I still cry.
I still miss you.

Why can't you be here with me?
It feels like nothing is left of our family.
Why can't you be here with me?
I don't want to always be alone.

Where have you been all my life?
I have grown up without you.
I have grown up in a troubled family.
And I've never been more on my own!

Would you be proud of our family?
Would you be proud of me?
I've made so many mistakes and I have been so very stupid.
Would you even be proud of who I've become?

Why can't you be here with me?
It feels like my life has always been broken into pieces.
My family feel like strangers to me and I feel completely broken.
Why can't you be here with me?
Why can't you make everything right in my life?

I feel lost in a dream of a vision of a perfect family and a perfect me.
I can't help but keep on missing you!
There is nothing I want more than for you to be here with me!

I keep on struggling to make this life I have worth living.
To find the strength and power to keep going.
It would be so much easier if you were here!

Why did you leave me all alone?
Left feeling broken and forgotten.
Struggling to keep fighting by myself.
Why are you not here?
Sometimes I can't help but feel that everything was perfect till I appeared.

Why did you have to go and leave me on my own?
Why did you have to go?

The Inside Look

Why couldn't you stay where you were and still are needed?

I still cry myself to sleep at night.
I'll always Miss You!

Finale Part 3: The Inner True Self

Open The Doors

I'm so sick of feeling locked out, boxed out and so far away from you.
I'm so sick of fighting, pleading and hoping for you to trust me.
I'm running out of things that I can do.
Don't keep locking me out, just let me in and together we can be free.

Open the doors and let me in you can always count on me.
Open the doors and let me see what is stopping you.
I will love you till the very end if you only let it be.
Open the doors and take a risk because I promise that my love is true.

I know you have your battles but I will fight for you.
I know you have your fears but so does everyone.
My love is true! All I want is you!

Open the doors and let me in I promise I'll always love you!
I know it's a risk but life's a gamble and we could win it all.
Open the doors and let me love you.
Open your heart and let me in I'm so tired of hitting a wall.

Even when I feel weak I will never stop fighting for your heart.
You're worth the wait and I'll never hesitate.
My love is true and if you allow it we will never be apart.
It won't be quick, but it's alright for you I'm willing to wait.

When you open the doors and let me in you will learn you can always count on me.
When you open the doors and let me see your truth I will always love you.
I will love you till the very end and soon you will see.
So when you open your heart and let me in I will always be here for you!

You Rock My World

Before you my life used to be so simple.
You have improved me little by little.
Before you my life used to be so dull.
A life once so empty but now forever full.

You were the light that pulled me through.
When no-one else knew what to do.
You held my hand and kept me strong.
Stood by my side no matter what I did wrong.

When I feel like I can't go on and there's nothing left of me.
It is you that I always see!
Your strength makes me feel strong.
To me you can do no wrong!

Without you I don't know where I would be.
Without you there would be no me.
Without you I would forever live in misery.

Even when I feel like I have no more strength I always have you to pull me through.
Even when I feel so lonely I always have you.
You rock my world and make me feel so good.
You stayed with me when no-one else would.
You rock my world and give me so much happiness.
You clean up my life when you know it's a mess.

A person like you is so hard to find.
Someone who is genuinely always kind.
You are full of fun and when needed you're always there.
Because of you I have nothing left to fear.

You are my strength and my truest friend.
You continue to rock my world and that will never end!

Together We Fall

Take my hand.
Together we will stand.
Forever side by side.

There's nothing that we can't do!
As long as we're together.
All I need is you.
You and I forever!

If we fall then we will fall together.
I will stay by your side forever.
Loving you comes easy to me.

I have never loved and I will never will again.
I will never love someone like I love you.
I can take of all life's struggles and all of the pain.
As long as I still have you.

Together We Stand!
Together We Fall!
Forever hand in hand.
We can have it all

Take What You Got

You've got to Take What You Got!
Whether you like it or not!
We only have one life to live!

So what if you may not have it all?
So what if you don't feel like a star?
There's no reason in life to why you can't have a ball.
You need to learn there is nothing wrong with who you are.

You've got to Take What You Got!
Whether you like it or not!
We only have one life to live!

You may feel at times like you are at the end of your road.
Like there is nowhere else for you to go.
There's always some way or someone to help you burden off your load.
You are worth so much more than what you already know.

Living your life is never easy, it's like an ongoing war.
But you've got to keep on fighting until you win.
Because you will learn to go far.
Once you learn never to give in.

You've got to Take What You Got!
Whether you like it or not!
We only have one life to live!

So let's all make the most of what we have got.
Don't ever let yourself be left behind.
Don't ever let yourself be forgot.
Life is always going to be hard, but there's always ways to unwind.

Once you learn and feel pride in who you are.
You will feel like a star.
No matter the pain, it will eventually go.
Trust me I should know.

You've got to Take What You Got!
Whether you like it or not!
We only have one life to live!

Ultimate Me

You can either love me or you can hate me.
But none of you even know me.

I'm the kind of guy who is never going to blend in!
I will never let anyone tell me who to be!
I will never stop because I'm always in it for the win!
We are all different! There is nobody out there like me!

My friends may mean a lot to me but I won't let anyone take me for a ride.
If you are good to me then maybe one day I will let you see what's inside.

I like to party away the pain.
I like to laugh away the troubles of yesterday.
Warning if you get too much of me I could drive you insane!
I'm going to get what I want and let nobody stand in the way!

Can't you all see?
This is the Ultimate Me!

I am not the kind of person to start trouble for anyone.
But if I have to, I will defend me until the end!
I may know how to have some fun.
But I also know when it should end!

Sometimes I don't always get seen in the brightest light.
Nobody is ever going to be perfect, although people love to act it.
The true events of my life could give some people a fright.
But in the end you will all see, that when it comes to my life I'm just making the most of it!

Can't you all see?
This is the Ultimate Me!

I'm anything but normal but I love to be this way.
Some people are going to tell you that I'm crazy, that I'm clinically insane.
But all I'm doing is learning how to live life like it's your very last day!

I've learned to smile even when the pain is killing me.
Because I know in the end it comes down to me to pull myself through.
Don't ever let yourself live a life in misery!
The only thing that has the power to stop your happiness is you!

Let them try and break me down!
Let them try and change who I am!
Let them try and make me frown!
I am always going to stay true to who I am!

Can't you all see?
This is the Ultimate Me!

Everyone should just let themselves be free!
Why should we even think twice about what people might say or see?
Everyone should be proud of who they are!
Because who you are is what has taken you so far!

Can't you all see?
This is the Ultimate Me!
This can be the Ultimate Us!
I don't care if they don't like what they see!
And neither should we!

About The Author

Dennis Alexander Prosser has been writing since a very young age starting his own fanfiction based short stories on Bebo at the age of 12 and publishing his first novel "Kentwood" two weeks before turning 17. A year later releasing the follow up "Kentwood Round Two" and a vampire novel called "Bite Me". Since his first three novels Dennis has been living rather quietly but recently returned to the writing world late last year with his online poetry blog "Dennis: An Inside Look Into The Madness" on blogger which has done fairly well since launching creating inspiration for this poetry book.

"Kentwood", "Kentwood Round Two" and "Bite Me" are available to buy at www.lulu.com

www.ingramcontent.com/pod-product-compliance
Ingram Content Group UK Ltd.
Pitfield, Milton Keynes, MK11 3LW, UK
UKHW041904190726
13854UKWH00003B/1076

9 781365 351433